Library of
Davidson College

Doughboy Doggerel

Doughboy Doggerel

Verse of the American Expeditionary Force 1918–1919

Alfred E. Cornebise, ed.

Ohio University Press
Athens, Ohio   London

Introduction and Notes © Copyright 1985 by
Alfred E. Cornebise.
Printed in the United States of America.
All rights reserved.

Library of Congress Cataloging in Publication Data

Main entry under title:

Doughboy doggerel.

  Bibliography: p.
  Includes index.
  1. World War, 1914-1918—Poetry. 2. American poetry—
20th century. 3. Soldiers' writings, American.
4. War poetry, American. I. Cornebise, Alfred E.
PS595.W63D68   811'.52'080358   85-10448
ISBN 0-8214-0798-8

Table of Contents

Introduction	vii
Section 1: Pride and Patriotism	1
Section 2: Sea Change: Over and Back	25
Section 3: How They Served and Soldiered	45
Section 4: Heroes All: The Honored Dead	61
Section 5: The Shores of Home	67
Section 6: Les Femmes	79
Section 7: Allies and Enemies	97
Section 8: The Lighter Side: Laughs and Levity	107
Section 9: A Miscellany	117

Introduction

"The Army's Poets are its true interpreters.... The Army's Poets are the spokesmen of the Army's soul." With these words *The Stars and Stripes,* the famous American soldier newspaper, drew attention to its doughboy poet contributors. Much of the poetry that the paper received in huge quantities from its readers was admittedly less than technically sound. Indeed, as the commentator went on to say, "Many a poem printed . . . limped along on crutches and [was] linked together with highly questionable rhymes." But this doggerel—for that, for the most part, was what it was—was not tampered with so as not to touch its essential sentiment, or "heart," which "this verse possesses as verse seldom possessed it before." Obviously, poetry expressing the deep feelings of its creators was felt to be a desirable thing, speaking of "the Army's longing and love for things and friends across the seas, of slum and cooties and mud; it speaks the Army's determination to see this through, to keep at this bitter and glorious business of war until the high aims for which it is fighting are achieved, when the Army's Poets in unison shall interpret the Army's soul in a paean of victory."[1]

Doughboy doggerel frequently reflected romanticism, a major characteristic of the American Expeditionary Forces (AEF), and of the land from whence they had sailed. These romantic, rather than realistic or naturalistic, outpourings of the popular mind, as opposed to the literary or academic mind, closely reflected America's mood. That temper was conditioned by several factors: for example, the influential nineteenth century American historians, such as Francis Parkman, George Bancroft, and William Prescott, wrote as romantics rather than as historians aspiring to follow Leopold von Ranke's insistence upon objectivity. Their major themes emphasized the triumph of liberty over tyranny, and the conquest of a continent. With the coming of the "splendid little war" against Spain at the end of the century, the crusade for liberty against absolutism was internationalized. At this juncture, one of absolutism's uglier manifestations appeared: the German Kaiser and his Reich. The New World, then, must save the Old from its bondage, since despite bitter conflict, the Allies seemed unable to win. So the nature of the crusade was set forth, with a naiveté concerning the rightness of America's institutions and ideals. This was usually expressed as the campaign to make the "world safe for Democracy," (sometimes rendered in the shorthand as "w. s. for D."). As the literary scholar Charles Genthe reminds us, "It took Americans a long time to mount their chargers, but when they did they set forth with a Calvinistic zeal fired by years of innocent isolationism befitting a young, naive Christian nation bent on moralizing 'corrupt' Europe."[2] When it seemed that America's entry was decisive, and when the absolutists, before too many months were out, were suing for armistices, the doughboys could perhaps be excused for some of their exuberance and their firm belief that America's role had been decisive. Patriotism was thus a common feature of much doughboy poetry.

There were religious dimensions to the crusade, and the average soldier had only contempt for the German claims on the same deity he worshipped. Accordingly, the famous German belt buckle emblazoned with "*Gott mit Uns*" became a favorite souvenir.

Much of the poetry revealed the religious aspects of the American involvement in Europe; and any fallen American knight was assured of his place immemorial in the remembrance of his buddies, loved ones, and the grateful nation. Thus, the Allied cause was a moral and religious one and a manifestation of God's will—the advancement of the best of Western Civilization and Christendom—which was clearly being accomplished in the struggle.

Then, too, there were the rescue and vindication of brutalized humanity; there was the need to carry the attack against the assaulters of defenseless women and children. Belgium was the best symbol of this need, though what the French had suffered was also widely recognized and appreciated by the Americans. This preoccupation reflects a common aspect of romanticism, an attempt to simplify and personify the forces of good and evil. Some of the poetry deals with this attempt.

In addition, the romantic doughboy extolled the virtues of heroes, and one should not scoff at those men in the rear areas who, finding their own contributions confined to mundane, dreary shuffling of papers and the materials of war, sought action at the front. Their feelings of guilt at being denied action resulted in a great quantity of poetry attempting to put as good a face as possible on this sad state of affairs. Expressions of pride that the men behind the men behind the guns were heroes in their own right, even if not recognized as such, prevailed though the envy of the frontline troops is sometimes imperfectly concealed. The fears of death or of being maimed were considered as nothing compared with the opportunity of participating in the exhilarating, uplifting experiences which the frontlines were said to provide.

The crusaders likewise had their views of womanhood. Many saw their lady loves at home in the ideal sense, especially their mothers. One scholar has correctly stated that the AEF "was an army whose newspapers printed poems on motherhood that would have made a later generation of soldiers snort or writhe with embarrassment."[3] However, women were not always seen as worthy of being placed on a pedestal, and the unfaithful girl back home was frequently commented on. The men themselves could be less than faithful, some succumbing to the charms of European women.

But the poetry of the doughboys reflected more than romanticism. Much of it was lighthearted banter and patter with attempts at humor. Crusaders, it says in effect, need not be altogether serious.

Other subjects that interested the men of the AEF, as revealed in their poetry, included the sea voyages involved, details of army life, and developments back home, especially the victory of the prohibitionists, almost universally deplored by the troops.

It is unfortunate that many people who learn about the Great War do so through the eyes of the disillusioned: through the pages of Remarque's *All Quiet on the Western Front;* Robert Graves' *Goodbye to All That;* or Hemingway's *Farewell to Arms,* fine as this literature is. While many doughboys later suffered misgivings, bitterness and disillusionment, it is instructive to attempt to encounter them as they were in 1918–1919, before the rot—or sanity—set in. Indeed, rather than being characteristic of that era, the spirit of disillusionment is much more characteristic of our own age. More than we are aware, we are strongly influenced by the consequences of the Treaty of Versailles, the rise of the totalitarian regimes, World War II, the Cold War, Korea, and Vietnam. Recognizing the truth of the statement that "the past is a foreign country; they do things differently there,"[4] we should seek to understand the doughboys in their own "foreign country." It is therefore necessary to take them at their own valuations; to take them and their words seriously; to accept what they said as authentic manifestations of their own feelings and not as so much cant or hypocrisy. As one scholar of the period reminds us, we should not indulge the sophisticated impulse or the cynical laugh when encountering the often-mouthed patriotic cliches and the melodrama of vaulting with fixed bayonet "over the top." These were no mere posturings; the doughboys meant all of them from the heart and the soul. The soldier-poets were sincere believers, and many of the thousands of American dead died believing in what they professed.[5]

Obviously, we are not here concerned with the Rupert Brookeses nor the Edmund Blundens. Their poetry has been—justifiably—frequently perused and thoroughly analyzed. The rhyming we're interested in is of another sort: that produced by men more poetasters than poets, who lacked the advantages of an Oxbridge education—rather those who were nurtured on the McGuffey Readers—not the works in the original of Greek poets. But men from New Jersey, Iowa and Kansas, after all, plodded through the same mud as, say, a Siegfried Sassoon. If their muse was not one of such dulcet tones as his, muse it was; and it inspired them to produce something quite like poetry if one is not over careful as to definition.

To be sure, while divergent backgrounds explain some of the differences between the lighter American verse and that of the British soldier-poets, which in the late war years was characterized by disillusionment and morbidity, there was another most important factor to be considered, the relatively short time that Americans were actually engaged in combat on a large scale. Though they were there earlier, it was not until the spring of 1918 that there were Americans in sufficient numbers in the lines to have an appreciable effect on the course of the war. By the summer, the Germans were in retreat. A heartening experience for the war-weary Allies, this evidence of Allied victory was positively exhilarating for the doughboys; and the war of movement, largely absent from the Western Front since 1914, reemerged, breaking the long-standing stalemate. The Armistice was then not long in coming. Though the American troops fought some sharp engagements, in certain instances sustaining heavy casualities, they were largely spared the long, dreary, grinding punishment of trench warfare. This experience had effectively destroyed the earlier romanticism of the British poets such as Brooke, Owen and others, whose poetic efforts early in the war also possessed the lighter touch. No doubt had the Americans been as long in the lines, they too would have changed their outlook, and their verse as well would have been affected.

Just why the doughboys so readily turned to rhyme is perhaps explained in part by their education, which even in the lower school grades emphasized verse. Then too, they read a great deal of the poetry of Robert Service, together with that of Kipling, these two writers being the favorite poets of the American men in France. In addition, the American newspapers that the men were accustomed to reading commonly published great quantities of verse, often on the front page. Now, they not only read a great deal of poetry, they wrote it by the ton, sending bales of poems to the editors of the military newspapers then being published, such as the famous *The Stars and Stripes*, the later *The Amaroc News* and numerous other troop newspapers that sprang up in that era. Much of the poetry was no doubt worked out more or less laboriously as to rhyme and meter. More poems were conceivably dashed off in a flash of inspiration, perhaps being born around the famous Sibley stove in some tent or hut, with one's comrades as midwives, with a good deal of mirth associated with the enterprise, with cleverness being recognized and rewarded with a kneeslap or a pat on the back. The results were soon on the way to an editor. Or the truck driver might have composed verse during long hours in a traffic jam or while traversing the long, sometimes strikingly beautiful, tree-lined white roads of France. A doughboy on a firestep in a trench suddenly thought of home and he sent in that direction, Mecca-like, a prayer of love and remembrance in poetic form which eventually found its way into a newspaper's pages. The flag, the sounds and smells of the camp, barracks, the tents or trenches, were suddenly evocative of something in one's past; a breeze sniffed engaged the mind, compelling its owner to record the impressions in verse. The moon still shone, after all; the imperatives of the natural world could not be denied. Even in the midst of hardest battle, the birds still sang, poignant reminders of life's persistency in the midst of destruction and decay. It was often remarked—even proverbial—that the flowers seemed to bloom most brilliantly on the battlefield, the beauty of the flowers fed by fetid flesh. The sense of fleeting life could not be denied either. These impressions, the sharpened senses in bodies hardened and disciplined, led to a quickening of mental effort and alertness, not always simply to the lockstep of military precision, all contributing to the acts of poetic creation.

Much of the poetry amounts to minimemoirs. While we

possess numerous diaries, memoirs, and autobiographies of the combatants in the Great War, countless thousands of the men closely engaged did not possess the skills, education, time or inclination to develop such sustained works. Odd moments in training, in troopships, in transit camps as members of casual units, in outfits at the front nervously awaiting action—these would lend themselves to poetic composition. The otherwise unknown men evoke in their lines much of the atmosphere of the Great Adventure. Thus Joseph Conrad's "obscure inner necessity" is, in their case, obscure no longer; it has surfaced for our instruction and edification.

The poetry is perhaps all the more useful in that it is often characterized by a heedless verve and vitality sometimes lacking in more formal work. There was not the hope—or fear—of posterity's judgments or of a favorable reception beyond that of one's doughboy peers. The appeal was not to the critics, but to one's buddies. Therefore, some poems, written in pedestrian language, were overly sentimental, yet evocative of the feelings of the author at the moment. Other poems, however, producing mood and setting with stirring images, can still move the reader.

The question remains: why inflict these upon the reading public? Is this emphasis on the *vox populi vox dei* idea a sound one? Is it a specifically useful one regarding poetry? Should we not let "sleeping doggerel lie"? The "convinced democrat" has no qualms about the matter. "He perceives a richness, a variety, a profusion, and an amplitude in popular literature that takes the individual reader out of his narrow routines and brings him into an awareness of humanity at large." So the well-known journalist and scholar Frank Luther Mott argued regarding the uses of popular literature in general. He continued: "He [the 'democrat'] thinks that such a literature has far more to tell the sociologist, the historian, the philologer, and even the philosopher and the artist, than the more precious compositions [of] the few."[6] In this way is posed once more the confrontation of the Platonic doctrine of *demos* versus excellence.

This emphasis upon history and literature from the bottom up is now enjoying considerable vogue. It is at least partially justified when one considers the ever widening gap between the professional historians and literati and the general public, and the meaning and value of much scholarly endeavor, which becomes less and less apparent and meaningful to the ordinary human beings who do not share the interests of professionals nor care about their interminable debates. Seeking knowledge and understanding at a level that they can comprehend, they turn to the experiences of the rank and file, the common life occurrences that they can relate to. Therefore, it can be argued that there is the need to return history and literature to the people at the risk, admittedly, of lowering its level to the "low brow," emphasizing, as in the case of this study, poetry of the immediate, even the crude.

The poetry that follows is drawn mainly from the World War I edition of *The Stars and Stripes* with a few selections from *The Amaroc News*. The former was published in Paris as an eight-page weekly beginning on 8 February 1918 and continuing to the issue of 13 June 1919. The latter was the daily newspaper of the American forces assigned after the Armistice to stations in the American occupation zone along the Rhine. Published in Coblenz, Germany, it first appeared on 21 April 1919, continuing to 24 January 1923, when the American troops were withdrawn.[7] The poems are presented in sections topically organized. The issue of the paper in which each appeared is indicated following each poem, together with the poet's name, if known. Each section is introduced with pertinent comment specifically describing the nature of the poetry contained therein.

Notes

1. *The Stars and Stripes* (Paris), issue of 16 August 1918.
2. Charles V. Genthe, *American War Narratives, 1917–1918. A Study and Bibliography* (New York: David Lewis, 1969), p. 11.
3. Fred Davis Baldwin, "The American Enlisted Man in World War I," (Ph.D. diss., Princeton, 1964), p. 198.
4. L.P. Hartley, in *The Go-Between*, as quoted in David E. Stannard, *Shrinking History* (New York: Oxford University Press, 1980), p. 117.
5. Genthe, *American War Narratives*, p. 6.
6. Frank Luther Mott, *Golden Multitudes. The Story of Best Sellers in the United States* (New York: R.R. Bowker and Company, 1947), p. 2.
7. For studies of each of these newspapers see this editor's *The Amaroc News. The Daily Newspaper of the American Forces in Germany, 1919-1923* (Carbondale: Southern Illinois University Press, 1981); *The Stars and Stripes: Doughboy Journalism in World War I* (Westport, Conn.: Greenwood Press, 1984).

1 Pride and Patriotism

Proportionally, perhaps more poems on pride were submitted to the editors of the various military newspapers than on any other single subject. There was pride expressed in the nation for at last having entered the war. There was similarly pride in the new army drawn as it was from all segments of the nation, burying regional and sectional differences, especially those lingering from the Civil War. To be sure, some regions might be excused a measure of self-praise if it were properly directed. A case in point is 2d Lt. Edward Magee's "New England Ambitions." The new American army sought to meld all creeds and social classes—if not yet all colors and races. Eventually two million men would be in France, about one-half of whom were committed to battle, a source of pride in itself. The ability of that army to make a "real man" out of a recruit—even if he were from the well-to-do classes—was frequently praised.

If the quantity of poetry is any measure, *The Stars and Stripes* seems to have had a strong sense of the relative importance of the various combatant arms. The infantry was regarded as the "Queen of Battles," and many poems gave infantrymen pride of place. However, the artillery likewise came in for considerable acclaim, especially praiseworthy being the famous French "75" light artillery piece so often mentioned in the literature of the war years, and which equipped many American units.

Among the new weapons were the tank and the aircraft, both of which received some attention from enthusiastic initiates into the mysteries associated with them. The poem "The Tank" was typical. Nevertheless, much of the army's transport was still accomplished by horse or mule-drawn conveyances, and artillery as well was pulled by animals, as the poem "The Driver" indicates.

In truth, it was the combined efforts of all arms which produced the success long sought, though most Americans felt that beyond question it was American efforts that tipped the balance on the battlefield, a conclusion that was officially frowned upon in the name of Allied unity. Lt. Grantland Rice, in his "The Third Army Responds," comments on American pride. As far as the rank and file were concerned, however, the issue was not whether the Americans won the war, but which outfits had been most instrumental in gaining the victory. The interesting poem "Trials of an M.P." focuses on some aspects of this subject always calculated to raise considerable controversy whenever it was broached. In any case, many men developed a taste for the soldier's life, one of whom seems to have been John S. Madden, if his poem "The Call of the Service" is any indication of his true feelings.

The New Army

Who are those soldiers
    Who go marching down?
They're the young fellows
    Of your old home town.

The butcher's son, the baker's,
    His Honor's lad, too;
The old casual mixture
    Of Gentile and Jew.

Don't they march manly!
    Ay, they step light;
And soon by the papers,
    Ye'll see they can fight!

> R. R. Kirk
> *The Stars and Stripes*
> (28 June 1918)

In Our Mess Hall

There's a cracker bold from Georgia and he's
    strong for Robert Lee,
A sport or two from dear old Herald Square;
Beside a Jersey skeeter sits a husk from Ten-
    nessee,
Who bunks with Bobby Jones from Delaware.
A Texas ranger loans his knife to Kane from
    Erin's Isle,
A kid from Carolina cuts the bread;
A limey from Australia is the first to crack a
    smile,
When bald-head Pete from Naples shows his
    head.

A tango-kid from Rector's* and a Hoosier chop
    the wood,
A chap from Pennsylvania serves the beans;
A two-gun man from Tucson says the "chow
    is roarin' good,"
And so does Jazz Band Joe from New Orleans.
The skipper hails from Oregon—out where the
    roses grow
And where the birds are singing all the time—

---

* A high-class supper club in New York City.

*In fact you'll find it just the same, no matter
    where you go,
From Maine 'way down to Dixie's sunny
    clime.*

>Sgt.-Maj. Howard A. Herty
>*The Stars and Stripes*
>(10 January 1919)

New England Ambitions

The German hordes are coming on,
　　Us Rubes will meet the Boche,*
And ere another day has gone,
　　They'll know we're here, b'gosh!

For though they number pretty strong,
　　We hope they all will come,
For then this scrap won't last so long,
　　We'll chaw 'em up, b'gum!

We'll show 'em that this gang of Rubes
　　Will not give in a speck;
We'll mix it with those German boobs,
　　Then goodbye, Boche, by heck!

Then when at last the peace is made,
　　They'll know that we're the ginks
That put the Kaiser in the shade,
　　New England guys, by jinks!

　　　　　　　　2d Lt. Edward L. Magee
　　　　　　　　The Stars and Stripes
　　　　　　　　(16 August 1918)

---

* Apparently the word *Boche* first appeared in about 1860, a low-class Paris slang word meaning a "bad lot." After the Franco-Prussian War of 1870–71, the term was generally applied to Germans in the former French province of Alsace as "Alboches" or "Allemands Boches" and in World War I to Germans in general.

The Plute

*He may be a plute in the circle back home, but it don't get him
      nothin' out here;*
*His belly may ache for a glass of champagne, but he's lucky as Hell to
      get beer.*
*His custom, you know, in the land of the free was to rise from his bed
      about nine—*
*A valet would dress him and button his shoes and bring him his
      breakfast and wine.*
But how things have changed since the draft sucked him in!—
      he rises at 6:30 now,
And, drinking black coffee, remarks on the fact he's walked
      half a mile for his chow.

*His sleep once was lulled by the sound of the storm as it whistled and
      roared round the house;*
*Perhaps he was wakened, but slumbered again, as snug and as warm
      as a mouse.*
But now he is billeted out in a barn on straw in an old cattle stall,
*While jack rabbits scampering over the field are seen through the holes
      in the wall.*
Oh, how things have changed since the draft sucked him in
      and cast his small world in dull gloom!
He shivers and shakes when a storm whistles now and blows
      all the snow in the room.

But think of the folks in the circle back home who sigh for the one that is gone;
They quickly forget what a nuisance he was and patiently wait for the dawn
Of the day that shall bring him from out of the war, and back to his comfort and ease;
They dream not how deep he has drunk of the cup, and the knowledge he's gained by degrees.
Oh, how things have changed since the draft sucked him in is told by his coating of tan;
He went as a number—and lo and behold! He comes to them now as a MAN.

>Sgt. Richard C. Colburn
>*The Stars and Stripes*
>(5 April 1918)

Mlle. Soixante-Quinze

Oh, mistress fit for a soldier's love
  Is the graceful 75;
As neat and slim, and as strong and trim
  As ever a girl alive.

Where the steel-blue sheen of her mail
    is seen,
  And the light of her flashing glance,
In the broken spray of the roaring fray
  Is the soul of embattled France.

Her love is true as the heaven's blue—
  She will fight for her love till death;
Her hate is a flame no fear can tame,
  That slays with the lightning's breath.

For the sun of day turns fogged and
    gray,
  And night is a reeling hell
When she swings the flail of the shrap-
    nel's hail,
  Or looses the bursting shell.

From high Lorraine to the Somme and
    the Aisne,

She has held at bay the Hun,
That with broken strength he may pay,
at length,
For the sins that his race has done.

For Alsace, torn from the mother land,
Ravished and mocked and chained;
For Belgium, nailed to the martyr's
cross,
For holding her faith unstained.

Thou Maid,* who cam'st, like a beacon
flame,
In thy people's darkest hour,
Who bade them thrill with patriot will
By the spell of thy mystic power.

As thou gav'st them heart to speed the
dart
From arquebus and bow,
Give us to drive, with the 75,
Our bolts on a baser foe.

That we who have come from Freedom's
home
Across the western wave,
Such blows shall give that France may
live
As once for us she gave.

* A reference to Jeanne d'Arc.

May our good guns play with a stinging
       spray
   On the Prussian ranks of war,
And smite them yet as did Lafayette
   The hireling Huns of yore!

May we aim again at a tyrant's men
     As straight and swift a blow
As at Yorktown came, with smoke and
       flame,
    From the guns of Rochambeau!*

Oh, a mistress fit for our soldier love
     Is the soixante-quinze, *our boast,*
Our hope and pride, like a new-won
       bride,
     But the dread of the Kaiser's host!

From the Golden Gate to the Old Bay
       State
    Our marching millions flow,
But the Girl of Gaul shall lead us all
    When victory's bugles blow!

                        Anon.
                        The Stars and Stripes
                        (26 April 1918)

---

* Comte de Rochambeau was a French general who greatly assisted the American colonists in the war for independence.

The Tank

*Oh, she's nothin' sweet to look at an' no sym-
                phony to hear;
        She ain't no pomp of beauty, that's a cinch—
She howls like Holy Jumpin' when a feller
                shifts a gear,
        But she's a lovey dovey in a pinch.
Just head her straight for Berlin and no matter
                what the road,
        Or whether it's just trenches, trees and mud,
And I'll guarantee she'll get there with her
                precious human load
        And her treads a-drippin' red with German
                blood,
                Oh, you tank! tank! tank!
                She's a pippin, she's a daisy, she's a
                        dream!
Where the star-shells are a-lightin' up the
        thickest of the fightin',
                She'll be sailin' like a demon through
                        the gleam.
If the way is rough and stony and the vantage
                point is far,*

*Just slip her into high and hang on tight,
Shove your foot down on the throttle and to
            hell with all the jar—
    She'll take you clean from here to out of
            sight.
Course you've got to clean and scrub her same
            as any piece of tin
    That's worth the smoke to blow her up the
            flue;
But just whisper to her gently, pat her back
            and yell "Giddap!"
And there ain't a thing she wouldn't do for
            you.
                Oh, you tank! tank! tank!
                    She's a Lulu, she's a cuckoo! She's the
                        goods!
When the Boches see you comin', they will set
            the air to hummin',
                    A wavin' of their legs to reach the
                            woods.
When the last great rush is over and the last
            grim trench is past,
    She will roll in high right through old Berlin
            town,
Her grim old sides a-shakin' and her innerds
            raisin' hob,
    Intent on runnin' Kaiser Wilhelm down,
Then she'll find him and we'll bind him to her*

grindin', tearin', treads,
And we'll start her rollin' on the road to Hell—
Shove her into high and leave her, tie her bloomin' throttle down,
We'll say she's lived her life and lived it well.
Oh, you tank! tank! tank!
She's a devil! She's a dandy! She's sublime!
When her grimy hide goes hurlin' through the dirty streets of Berlin
Watch the goose step change to Yankee double time!

Sgt. Richard C. Colburn
The Stars and Stripes
(21 June 1918)

The Driver

I'm a slouch and a slop and a sluffer,
  And my ears they are covered with hair,
And I frequent inhabit the guardhouse—
  I'll be "priv" until "fini la guerre."
But off my horse, she shines like a countess,
  And my nigh made the general blink,
And they pull like twin bats fresh from Hades,
  And they're quick as a demimonde's wink.

Oh, it's often I'm late at formations
  And it's taps I completely disdain,
And my bunk, it brings tears from the captain,
  And the cooties are at me again.
But when there's a piece in the mire,
  With her muzzle just rimming the muck,
Then it's hustle for me and my beauties—
  If they don't they are S. O. of luck.*

And when there's some route that's receiving
  Its tender regards from the Huns,
Then we gallop hell bent for election
  To our duty o' feeding the guns.
The gas, the H. E.,† and the shrapnel,

---

* SOL stood for a common doughboy obscenity "shit out of luck."
† H.E. stood for high explosives.

They brighten our path as they burst,
But they've never got me or my chevals—
They'll have to catch up to us first.

I'm a slouch, and a slop and a sluffer,
And my ears they are covered with hair,
And I frequent inhabit the guardhouse—
I'll be "priv" until "fini la guerre,"
But my horses, they neigh when I'm coming,
An' my sarge knows how hefty they drag,
An' the cap, lent me ten francs this mornin'—
Here's to him an' to me an' the flag!

                Anon.
                The Stars and Stripes
                (28 June 1918)

The Third Army Responds*

To those who turn our way
Across the distant route—
To those who count each day
Unheeding Time doles out—
To those who watch and wait
Beyond the sea-girt span—
Whose dreams still hold the Western Gate—
Gentlemen—Our Clan!

To that which overhead
Now flutters at the Rhine—
Whose ripping rolls of red
Still shield the Staff and Line—
Whose glory is no wraith
From lowland up to crag—
Heart-emblem of our final faith—
Gentlemen—The Flag!

To those who may not take
The great ship, homeward bound—
To those in Honor's wake
Who hold the silent mound—
Who, by the cross-marked sword,

* The Third Army was the AEF outfit stationed in the American zone of occupation in Germany, with headquarters at Coblenz on the Rhine.

Stained hills and valleys red—
Who stay to keep eternal guard—
Gentlemen—Our Dead!

> Lt. Grantland Rice
> *The Stars and Stripes*
> (10 January 1919)

Trials of an M.P.

"Who won the war?" This battle-cry
They shout at me as they pass by
From box-car doors, and at a glance,
I have them placed—three weeks in France—
Unwashed, unkempt, replacements all,
Corn-willie fed, and so they bawl
Their rage at me as they rush past,
A dandy bunch to dare to ask
    Who won the war?

"Who won the war? The brave M.P's"
A drunken soldier flings the wheeze
And so he's pinched. I'm rather sore;
"What outfit Jack?" "The Q. M. Corps"*
I have to laugh, but on I lead,
He sobers up and stalls and pleads,
But no avail, so on we go
Up to the Cap who'll let him know
    Who won the war.

"Who won the war?" He's in a crowd,
And shouts it out so very loud
That you would think that he must be

---

* The Quartermasters normally performed their functions well back of the fighting.

The winner of a D.S.C.†
But guess again; he's too afraid
To show his face, and so he stayed
Back out of sight; the cowardly stiff
Dares not come out and ask me if
    We won the war.

"Who won the war?" He asks it low,
I turned around to let him know,
And then he laughs. "How are you, pal,
How can I get to Rue du Vall?"
A doughboy buck just back on leave,
With wounds and years shown on his sleeves,
I set him right, I'll tell you why
I can't get peeved; here is the guy
    Who won the war.

                    Anon.
                    The Stars and Stripes
                    (2 May 1919)

---

* The D.S.C.—Distinguished Service Cross—was one of America's highest decorations.

The Call of the Service

I said I was through with the service—
I'd forget the old life which I knew,
So I bought me a suit of civilians,
Socks, hat and everything new,
Then purchased a ticket for Frisco,
And say, for a time it was swell,
But somehow of late I get lonely,
And the feeling I have, well it's hell!

I was standing today down on Market,*
Right near where it crosses on Third,
When over the roar and the clamor,
The sound of a bugle I heard.
And a thrill seemed to grip and to hold me,
Ah, it's something I can't just explain,
But I knew that the lure of the service,
Was calling me back once again.

Then down through the streets of the city,
Came the close, serried ranks in review,
While over them streaming in splendor,
Was our flag, the old Red, White and Blue.
And a lump seemed to rise in my throat, Sir,

---

*   Market Street was one of San Francisco's main thoroughfares.

And my eyes, they were misty with tears.
Why I had to pull off my hat, Sir,
And swing it aloft with a cheer.

I forgot that I had on civilians,
That came from a fashionable store.
I forgot that I had an engagement,
With a belle down in Cherry's at four,
For my heart went right out with those boys, Sir,
As they marched past with firm measured tread,
And, somehow I thought of my buddy,
Whom I left over there with the dead.

Just a kid, but none, Sir, were braver,
And a soldier you bet, every inch,
The kind that will split fifty-fifty,
Whenever his pal's in a pinch.
Just a kid but the heart of a hero,
Throbbed under his olive drab breast,
Now I'm not at all strong on this sob stuff,
But I wept when my Buddy went West.

Three months I have been a civilian,
And I've mixed with the men of the town,
But I found no one in a hurry,
To reach out a hand when you're down,
This thing they call friendship is shallow,
If you haven't the coin it's a sham,

And I want to get back with the colors
And touch elbows again with a man.

I know I once hated the bugle,
That roused me from slumbers in bed,
I know I've cursed out all the non-coms
And wished that the captain was dead.
I served my full time in the kitchen,
As K. P. with Sergeant Bill,
But the call of the service has got me,
And I want to go back, and I will.

                         John S. Madden
                         The Amaroc News
                         (7 September 1919)

2 Sea Change: Over and Back

The voyage to Europe and back was the common experience of most members of the American Expeditionary Forces. The trip over marked the first time that many of the troops had seen the ocean. Indeed, the passage over could be a daunting, if thrilling experience, particularly dangerous because of the feared U-boats. However, not a soldier was lost to the subs on the voyages over. More probable was the danger of becoming seasick. The "Rime of the Prairie Mariner" well illustrates this. However, the nausea-producing waves exhilarated some of the soldiers, and more than one was inspired to compose poetry to the rhythm of the waves beating against troopships. Fra Guido was an example. Certainly one of the most exuberant was Pvt. Stewart Emery, who kept a "poetic log" of his journey to France. *The Stars and Stripes* later published several of his contributions. His poems reflecting the comradeship of shared thrilling experiences could speak for all men who have sailed off to wars through the centuries. To be sure, not all of the men left home lightheartedly, as one army poet recounts in his poem "Camouflage," a term which gained popularity at this time.

Soon the men lost some of their initial enthusiasm for the voyage, and the first glimpses of Europe, and the later first trip to the trenches for those who proceeded that far, were new attractions. But subsequently, the sea claimed their attentions once more as almost immediately following the signing of the

Armistice the men turned their faces, almost in unison as though on command, toward home. They now entered upon a new ordeal—waiting for the ships to take them back, while suffering the agonies of homesickness. Both *The Stars and Stripes* and *The Amaroc News* published a great number of poems on this theme, at the same time urging patience. The problems in getting the men home were numerous and formidable. In the first place, the Armistice was not a definitive peace treaty, for hostilities could be resumed; a large force must therefore be retained in Europe, at least for a time. Second, many men were required to occupy the American zone in Gemany. Finally, the logistical problems in shipping home some two million men were considerable and required many months to work out. Finding the large number of ships required was difficult; they simply were not immediately available.

Then there were the bad conditions at the notorious camps located around the ports. Many men dreaded being detained, especially when numbers of those collected there became victims of the flu, now in epidemic proportions both in Europe and in the United States. Such a delay became another ordeal to be borne on the way home, another gauntlet to be run. Lt. Grantland Rice, in his poem "Song of St. Nazaire," sought to encourage the troops, pointing out that once past the ports, they could look to the shores of home and the ending of their military service.

In any event, not only their experiences in Europe but also the voyages over and back worked "sea changes" on the men of the AEF, remaining a part of that Great Adventure which they would never forget, a part which, for good or ill, deeply altered their lives.

Rime of the Prairie Mariner

        He came all the way from Kansas
        Did the hero of these stanzas,
Where the land is largely—very largely
    flat,
        And his ante-bellum notion
        Of a topsy-turvy ocean
Was a puddle you could hide beneath
    your hat.

        Just before the transport started
        And for Overseas departed,
He was sure he'd have a safe and speedy
    trip,
        But to ward off every sickness
        He wore socks of extra thickness,
Though he carried nothing heavy on his
    hip.

        But his pains were unavailing,
        For he hung upon the railing
From the moment they were out of sight
    of land—
        It was not a time for laughter—

> *And for quite a while thereafter*
> *He had nothing on his stomach but his*
> *hand.*
>
> *When he started convalescing,*
> *He resumed his daily messing*
> *Without fearing every wavelet's rise*
> *and fall,*
> *But where'er the vessel drifted,*
> *Still the scene was never shifted—*
> *Just a circle full of water—that was all.*
>
> *Then he thought of Kansas prairies*
> *And his Susies and his Marys,*
> *And he groaned in utter anguish and*
> *despair:*
> *"We've been moving every minute,*
> *But there's something phoney in*
> *it—*
> *'Cause the gol-darned boat ain't getting*
> *anywhere!"*

Anon.
The Stars and Stripes
(28 June 1918)

"Let's Go"

Let's go, boys, let's go;
Let's go to strike for freedom's right.
Let's go to down the creed of might;
What matter if our youth we give,
If but exalted truth will live?
What matter if young blood is spilt,
When on our bodies will be built
The temple of eternal peace,
And strife 'mongst men forever cease?
Let's go, boys, let's go.

Let's go and teach barbarity
The milestones of humanity,
And curb the last great tyrant's greed
Until each man on earth is freed.
Let each man dedicate his soul
To liberty's immortal goal,
And give the world a finer birth—
To men good will, and peace on earth.

Lets go, boys, let's go;
On freedom's frontiers heroes fall,
And "Carry on!" to us they call.

What matter if perchance we die—
The quest is long, the dream is high;
Let's go the glory-day to gain,
When Brotherhood 'mongst men will
　　reign;
The bugles call, the drum-taps roll.
Let's go with cheer and daring soul—
Let's go, boys, let's go.

　　　　　　　　　　Fra Guido
　　　　　　　　　　The Stars and Stripes
　　　　　　　　　　(30 August 1918)

Transport Days

Old transport days, no, I'll never regret 'em,
 Days when this life seemed too good to be true,
Blue afternoons, will I ever forget 'em?
 Watching the combers slide by in review.
Sunshine and laughter and long, lazy napping,
 Curled on the deck while the planking was hot,
Bow wash for lullaby soothingly slapping
 World and its worriments all gone to pot.

We had the wonders of ocean at dawning,
 Ours were the glories of sunsets astern,
Tang of the spray on the lips in the morning,
 Nights, black as jet, where the star candles burn.
Pals to be proud of made better the jesting,
 Comrades of voyage and partners in chance,—
Those were the days of a golden, glad questing,
 Old transport days on the sea road to France.

> Pvt. Stewart Mackie Emery
> *The Stars and Stripes*
> (30 August 1918)

Sea Stuff

Now I'm a soldier, so I ain't
    No hand at art, but say,
There's things at sea I'd like to paint
    Before I'm tucked away.

A cruiser on the sunrise track,
    Alert to find the morn,
With every funnel belching black
    Into the red, gold dawn;

A line o' transports, crazy lined,
    On blue-green waves advance,
That sink their bows, all spray an' dewed,
    Hellbootin' it for France;

A manned gun peerin' out to port
    As evenin' shadows close;
Beyond, a ship slipped up an' caught
    Against a cloud o'rose;

A crow's nest loomin' from below
    Across the Milk Way's bars,

Just like a cradle rockin' slow,
  An' sung to by the stars.

No, I can't paint the things I've seen
  While we were passin' by,
But, all the same, they sure have been
  Worth lookin' at, say I.

> Pvt. Stewart Mackie Emery
> *The Stars and Stripes*
> (16 August 1918)

Our Chance

Gray sea, gray sky, and ships of mottled hue;
Gray sky, gray seas, yet cloud-rift bits of blue.
Gray mists, gray rain—beyond, the coasts of
    France,
Across the silent danger zone where we must
    take our chance.
We take our chance—a thousand eyes on each
    ship scan the sea,
Watching, waiting, watching for the crest of the
    Valkyrie;*
The crest of the Teuton goddess, the chooser of
    the slain,
Whose lone eye peers from the top of the sea
Where her victims' bones are lain.
We take our chance, clear-eyed, hearts high,
Sons of the Newer Day.
To drive the spawn of the Elder Gods back to
    their holes of clay.
We take our chance for the love of Christ,
Fighting the heathen horde;
We take our chance for the same high cause that
The blood of our grandsires poured.

* A reference to the conning tower of a submarine.

Gray seas, gray sky and the gathering dark
  before;
Gray sky, gray seas but beyond—the Gallic
  Shore!
Beneath the flag of Liberty, thank God, we take
  our chance.
On, on swift ships, on, on, brave men—
        Beyond's the coast of France!

                Anon.
                The Stars and Stripes
                (16 August 1918)

Camouflage

They tell us tales of camouflage,
The art of hiding things;
Of painted forts and bowered guns
Invisible to wings.
    Well, it's nothing new to us,
    To us, the rank and file;
    We understand this camouflage
    —We left home with a smile.

We saw the painted battleships
And earthen-colored trains,
And planes the hue of leaden skies
And canvas-hidden lanes.
    Well, we used the magic art
    That day of anxious fears;
    We understand this camouflage
    —We laughed away your tears.

They say that scientific men
And artists of renown
Debated long on camouflage
Before they got it down.
    Well, it came right off to us,

We didn't have to learn;
We understood this camouflage
—We said we'd soon return.

We understand this camouflage,
This art of hiding things;
It's what's behind a soldier's jokes
And all the songs he sings.
Yes, it's nothing new to us,
To us, the rank and file;
We understand this camouflage
—We left home with a smile.

Anon.
The Stars and Stripes
(28 June 1918)

Homesickness

Gotta be a soldier. Gotta stick t' biz—
Gotta keep on marchin' while the marchin' is;
    Gotta keep salutin';
        Gotta keep in trim;
    Bugle keeps on tootin',
        Home looks mighty dim.
    Gotta keep on stitchin',
        Gotta foller like a lamb—
    But, boy, my feet am itchin'
        For th' feel of Alabam'.
Gotta answer reveille. Gotta stand retreat;
Gotta be K. P. sometimes—soldiers has t'eat;
    Gotta keep a-workin'
        Jes' like there was war;
    Ain't no time for shirkin'
        Lots o' jobs in store;
    Ain't no time for switchin;
        Er lettin' things go slam—
    But, boy, my feet am itchin'
        Fer the feel of Alabam'.
Mammy writes she's "waitin' with a possum pie,"
My doggone mouth keeps waterin' till my throat is dry.
    Watermelon's handy—

Sugar cake am hot—
Enclosin' love from Mandy—
An' yet a feller's got
T' sweat here in a kitchen—
It's all fer Uncle Sam,
But, boy, my feet's sure itchin'
Fer the feel of Alabam'.
Sometimes, my lips get twitchin'—
Baby, that I am—
But, boy, my feet's done itchin'
Fer the feel of Alabam'.

Cpl. E. Rutherford, Jr.
The Stars and Stripes
(27 December 1918)

(Untitled)

I want to go home; I am tired of staying
    Where people don't savvy my tongue,
Where I cannot tell what the waiters are
      saying
    Nor know just how much I am stung.
I want to go back where I needn't climb
      stairways
    Or grope to my room in the gloom.
Or shiver in chambers like chill glacial air-
      ways,
        I gaze on the track to,
        I long to go back to,
That better and greater place, swift ele-
      vator place,
Hot radiator place—
          Home!
I want to go home; I am tired of getting
    This fancy but camouflaged food,
Pale substitute eats in a Frenchified set-
      ting—
    My tastes grow voracious and crude.
I'm dreaming of meals without food-card
      restrictions,

With much more of bodyless foam,
Where sugar and pastry meet no interdic-
            tions,
        I dream of and yearn to,
        I pant to return to,
That thrilling-to-utter land, makes-my-
            heart-flutter land,
Milk-fat-and-butter land—
            Home!

> Anon.
> *The Stars and Stripes*
> (6 June 1919)

Song of St. Nazaire

*Hurry on, you doughboys, with your rifle and
     your pack;
Bring along your cooties with your junk upon
     your back;
We'll house you and delouse you and we'll douse
     you in a bath,
And when the boat is ready you can take the
     Western Path.*

      *For it's home, kid, home—when you
          slip away from here—
     No more slum or reveille, pounding in
          your ear;
     Back on clean, wide streets again—
     Back between the sheets again
     Where a guy can lay in bed and sleep
          for half a year.*

*Hurry on, you lousy buck, for your last advance;
You are on your final hike through the mud of
     France;
Somewhere in the Good Old Town, you can
     shift the load,
Where you'll never see again an M. P. down the
     road.*

> *For it's home, boy, home, with the old*
> *   ship headed west;*
> *No more cooties wandering across your*
> *   manly chest;*
> *No more M. P.'s grabbing you—*
> *No more majors crabbing you—*
> *Nothing for a guy to do except to eat*
> *   and rest.*

Move along, you Army, while the tides are on
    the swell.
Where a guy can get away and not the S. O. L.
Where the gold fish passes and the last corned
    willy's through.
And no top sergeant's waiting with another job
    to do.

> *For it's home kid, home—when the*
> *   breakers rise and fall—*
> *Where the khaki's hanging from a*
> *   nail against the wall—*
> *Clean again and cheerful there—*
> *Handing out an ear full there—*
> *Where you never have to jump at the*
> *   bugle's call.*

        Lt. Grantland Rice
        The Stars and Stripes
        (2 May 1919)

3 How They Served and Soldiered

Many matters interested members of the Expeditionary Force such as what they wore and what they ate. One of the early casualties of the war was the old campaign hat. While not banned entirely, it was soon a rarity in Europe, certainly not appearing in the combat zones. But its loss was regarded as a major blow by many of the men, especially when it was replaced by the universally detested "overseas" or "forage" cap. Numerous poems addressed this deplorable development, and the one by 1st Lt. Fairfax Downey is particularly evocative of the prevalent attitudes on the subject.

The doughboys were naturally concerned with their chow, and many poems discussed military cuisine. Especially hated were "corned willie," or canned corned beef, and other dishes such as "slum," "monkey meat," and the similarly cordially detested salmon, universally called "goldfish." Even the officers felt on occasion that they were eating all of the animals to be found in any self-respecting zoo.

There were other things to endure. The louse—or cootie—was one of the best known nuisances of the Great War. He seems to have afflicted everyone no matter of what rank or station. Full-scale delousing operations were required, and much of the energy of the Medical Corps was expended in attempting to cope with the hated bug.

There were other things to suffer and endure, other dimensions of military service familiar to the doughboy poets who apparently omitted few of them in their musings. At least one soldier—surely there were others—hated to go on guard. Thousands deplored the lack of proper billets, especially early in the career of the AEF, when barracks and other housing were in short supply. Many men had to use makeshift accommodations, such as those mentioned in "the stable barns of France." All soldiers from their earliest army experience knew what "fall in" meant. Was this henceforth to be a permanent fact of life? Sgt. A. W. Bowen feared as much.

By Way Of Farewell

The war of the Trojans and all the
  Greek crew
Was fought for the sake of a fair lady
  who
Went absent without leave, for weal or
  for woe,
And took her permission *[leave] to Paris to go.*

All Greeks grasped steel helmets and
  trench knives and tanks
And wheel teams and chariots and fell
  into ranks.
Shipping boards gave no trouble with
  quarrels or slips:
The beauty of Helen had launched all
  the ships.

All cautioned their sweethearts that
  since they must go,
To keep home hearths heated, on flirt-
  ing go slow;
For each warrior was off to the battle
  and strife

To make the world safe for a good-
    looking wife.

But they'd never have fought if they'd
    read Helen's note,
Which just before leaving she hastily
    wrote:
"Menelaus just entered our once happy
    home
With an overseas cap *on the top of his*
    dome!"

1st Lt. Fairfax D. Downey
The Stars and Stripes
(31 May 1918)

A Subsistency

O compound of wrecked flesh, rent and torn
*   asunder,*
How do we e'er digest thy potency, I wonder—
Cold, killed cattle pounded into paste,
Pressed into tins and shipped to us in haste.
Greedily we eat thee, hot or cold or clammish,
How welcomely thou thuddest in the mess tins
*   of the famished.*
O leavings of a jackal's feast, O carrion sub-
*   lime,*
No matter how we scoff at thee, we eat thee
*   every time,*
Ah, CORNED WILLIE.

> Sgt. H. W. White
> *The Stars and Stripes*
> (26 July 1918)

Ballad of Officers' Mess

*The officers' mess
Was wont to guess
What kind of meat
They had to eat.
But none could tell
Just what the deuce
Was on that plate
'Midst all the juice.*

*It might be pork,
It might be stork,
Or alligate,
Or equine skate,
Frog, ape or ram,
None cared a fig;
When hungry, one
Just starts to dig.*

*The colonel swore
'Twas deadly boar;
The major swears
He's tasted hares;
We second lieuts.*

Could sure have told,
But we ate last—
The scent was cold.

Our wagers rough
On meat so tough
All came to naught,
As well they ought.
Here ends my yarn—
No bets went through;
It wasn't fair—
They had a zoo!

                          Anon.
                          The Stars and Stripes
                          (5 April 1918)

If I Were a Cootie

If I were a cootie (pro-Ally, of course),
I'd hie me away on a Potsdam-bound* horse,
And I'd seek out the Kaiser (the war-maddened
*   cuss),*
And I'd be a bum cootie if I didn't muss
His Imperial hide from his head to his toe!
He might hide from the bombs, but I'd give him
*   no show!*
If I were a cootie, I'd deem it my duty
To thus treat the Kaiser,
*   Ah, oui!*

And after I'd thoroughly covered Bill's area,
I'd hasten away to the Prince of Bavaria,
And chew him a round or two—under the
*   Linden—*
Then pack up my things and set out for old
*   Hinden.†*
(Old Hindy's the guy always talking 'bout
*   strafing)*
To think what I'd do to that bird sets me
*   laughing!*
If I were a cootie, I'd deem it my duty

* Sans Souci Palace, one of the Kaiser's main abodes, was at Potsdam.
† Field Marshal Paul von Hindenburg was head of the German General Staff.

To thus treat the Prince and old Hindy,
  Ah, oui!

I'd ne'er get fed up on Imperial gore—
I might rest for a while, but I'd go back for
    more.
I'd spend a few days with that Austrian crew,
And young Carl* himself I'd put down for a
    chew.
There'd be no meatless days for this cootie, I
    know,
They'd all get one jolly good strafing or so.
For if I were a cootie, I'd deem it my duty
To thus treat their damships,
      Ah, oui!

> Sgt. A. P. Bowen
> *The Stars and Stripes*
> (1 November 1918)

---

* Charles I, who ruled Austria-Hungary from 1916 to 1918, was the last Hapsburg to reign.

On Guard

I've done some dirty diggin', and I've toted heavy loads,
  I've marched for many miles a day on slimy, muddy roads;
I've loaded trucks, and chopped up wood, and thought it mighty hard,
  But I'd sooner do them all at once than have to go on guard.

They worked me in the kitchen till it tried my utmost soul,
  And then I joined the firing squad—the one that shovels coal.
I've even picked up stumps and scraps around the barracks yard,
  But I'd sooner do it all again than have to go on guard.

It's on those bitter, wintry nights—your backbone all a-chill,
  And cursin' every German boob, and mostly Kaiser Bill,
'Tis then you know within your soul there's nothing quite so hard
  As being routed out of bed to have to go on guard.

It's being out alone at night, and walkin' up and down,
  And speakin' not a word until the sergeant comes aroun',
And all the time a-thinkin' of your Susies or your Maud—
  Yep! I'd sooner do most anything than have to go on guard.

Sgt. H. J. Watson
The Stars and Stripes
(22 March 1918)

Billets

Dedicated to the gallant peasants of sunny France, who own them, and the officers of the A.E.F., who made the selection for the proletariat.

I've slept with horse and sad-eyed cow,
 I've dreamed in peace with bearded goat,
I've laid my head on the rusty plow,
 And with the pig done table d'hote.
I've chased the supple, leaping flea
 As o'er my outstretched form he sped,
And heard the sneering rooster's crow
 When I chased the rabbit from my bed.
I've marked the dog's contented growl,
 His wagging tail, his playful bite;
With guinea pig and wakeful owl
 I've shared my resting-place at night,
While overhead, where cobweb lace
 Like curtains drapes the oaken beams,
The spiders skipped from place to place
 And sometimes dropped in on my dreams.
And when the morning, damp and raw,
 Arrived at last as if by chance,
I've crawled from out the rancid straw
 And cussed the stable barns of France.

And sometimes when the day is done
 And lengthening shadows pointing long,

I dream of days when there was sun
 And street cars in my daily song.
But over here—ah! what a change,
 The clouds are German-silver lined—
Who worries when we get the mange?
 What boots it if our shoes are shined?
The day speeds by and night again
 Looms up a specter grim and bare;
We trek off to the hen house then
 And climb the cross barred ladder there—
Another biologic night
 Spent in a state sans *peace,* sans *sleep;*
And as I soothe some stinging bite,
 I mark the gentle smell of sheep,
The smell that wots of grassy dell,
 Of hillsides green where fairies dance.
The vision's past. . . . I'm back in Hell—
 An ancient stable barn of France.

We've slept with all the gander's flock,
 By waddling duck we've slumbered on—
In fact, we've slept with all the stock,
 And they will miss us when we're gone.
We've seen at times the nocturne eyes
 Of playful mouse on evening spree,
And the coastwise trade at night he plies
 With Brother Louse on a jambouree.
We've scratched and fought with foe unseen,
 And with the candle hunted wide

For the bug that thrives on Paris green,
    But cashes in on bichloride.*

Perchance may come a night of stars,
    Perchance the snow drift through the tile,
Perchance the evil face of Mars
    Peeks in and shows his wicked smile;
'Tis then we dream of other days
    When we were free and in the dance,
And followed in the old time ways
    Far from the stable barns of France.

                      Anon.
                      The Stars and Stripes
                      (19 July 1918)

---

* Paris green was a bright green powder used as an insecticide. Many doughboys felt it made bugs thrive rather than die. Bichloride—mercuric chloride—was apparently more effective, causing bugs to "cash in their chips," i.e., to die.

Line Up! Fall In!

I wonder if, when I get home
To wear a derby on my dome
And strut around in civvy pants,
I'll e'er get o'er the ways of France—
This army style that's always been:
For everything, Line Up! Fall In!

  Line up to simply holler "Here!"
    Fall in to show them why,
  Line up to get your issue stuff,
    Fall in for what you buy;
  Line up to get your army chow,
    Fall in to bed, and then
  Get ready to turn out next day
    And do it all again!

I went to Paris for a rest
From all such stuff (I thought it best),
Quoth I, "In bangup style I'll go
(No '40 Hommes or 8 Chevaux'),
To premiere classe I'll climb aloft
And bounce along on cushions soft."

> Line up to have your pass stamped out,
> > Fall in to board your train,
> And when, at last, you reach Paree,
> > Line up, get off again!
> Fall in to have your pass stamped in
> > And read a lot of con.
> Line up for Metro tickets and
> > Fall in to be stamped on!

"Ah, well," I sighed, "right here's the Y,
Now for a bed—tonight I'll lie
On linen sheets, not O. D. wool.*
Sir, please, a room, if they're not full,
And you don't mind if I turn in—"
"Ah, no," quoth he, "Right there! Fall in!"

> Line up for room and bed and board,
> > Fall in for all you lack,
> Line up to check your pack or bag.
> > Fall in to get it back;
> Line up to find out where to go,
> > Fall in to find out when
> Your train leaves Paris, then line up
> > To get stamped out again!

I wonder if, when I get home
To wear a derby on my dome
And strut around in civvy pants,

---

* Olive drab wool blankets of government issue, warm but hardly soft.

I'll find things there as here in France!
And if 'twill be, as it has been
For everything, Line Up! Fall in!

> *Line up to greet the folks and girl,*
>   *Fall in for civvy life,*
> *Line up to get your old job back,*
>   *Fall in to get a wife;*
> *And when you quit this vale of woe*
>   *To pass to realms on high,*
> *Line up to catch your death of cold,*
>   *Fall in, at last, to die!*

Sgt. A. W. Bowen
The Stars and Stripes
(9 May 1919)

4 Heroes All: The Honored Dead

The business of war invariably exacts its toll of life. The high calling of the Crusade was not proof against dead crusaders. Neither did euphemisms such as "gone West" or "over the top—to his rest" hide the hard facts of death. The poem "The Ward At Night" graphically highlights how many of the men died. But the troops had to deal with the tragedy and reverently commemorated their dead. Numerous tributes appeared, being especially numerous around Memorial Day in both *The Stars and Stripes* and *The Amaroc News*. A particularly compelling piece appearing on one such occasion was "Les Clycines," referring to the wisteria and its blooming a second time in autumn, after its spring blossoming, a fit symbol for remembrance. But while recognizing the demands of the hour and the claims of the service on the soldiers, an anonymous poet in his "Goodbye, Old Pal" was far more realistic as to the magnitude of the sacrifice of the dead. His reference to the graves of the fallen as a permanent trench against the Hun pointed to America's involvement in World War II as well.

One of the best known casualties of the war was Sgt. Joyce Kilmer, the celebrated "tree poet." A member of Headquarters Company, 165th Infantry, of the 42nd Division, Kilmer was killed in action on 30 July 1918. An unknown doughboy poet appropriately remembered him when the 69th paraded in his honor.

The Ward At Night

The rows of beds,
Each even spaced,
The blanket lying dark against the sheet,
The heavy breathing of the sick,
The fevered voices
Telling of the battle
At the front,
Of Home and Mother.

A quick, light step,
A white-capped figure
Silhouetted by the lantern's flame,
A needle, bearing sleep
And sweet forgetfulness.
A moan—
Then darkness, death.
God rest the valiant soul.

                                        Anon.
                                        The Stars and Stripes
                                        (29 November 1918)

Les Clycines*

"To those who bravely suffer, memory is kind. The wisteria when summer has burned away the last leaf, blooms again in Autumn more beautiful than ever."
Old French Saying

The wisteria is withered
That was purple by our doorway
On that fearsome, springtime morning
    Sweetheart, when you marched away.
Now the walls are drab and ugly,
And our hedgeway parched and dusty;
Summer mocks the tear-sweet picture
    Of our last, glad, wistful day.

But as sure as laughing Maytime
Stole you from me, Soldier-Lover,
Took the purple from my doorway,
    Left my heart a weeping tomb,
So will Autumn bring the mem'ry
Of your gentle, strong caresses,
Bring you, too—I have the promise—
    The wisteria's second bloom.

        Anon.
        The Stars and Stripes
        (30 May 1919)

* The French word for wisteria.

Goodbye, Old Pal

Goodbye, old Pal.
I've been to hell and back again;
There's where you fell, in mud, in blood, and
            rain.
Sure, we won—you paid the bill;
You swapped your life for that green hill;
    Goodbye, old Pal.

Goodbye, old Pal.
We're sailing home, our job is done;
But still your grave's a trench against the Hun.
Call us back; we'll make our stand
Where you keep guard in No Man's Land.
    Goodbye, old Pal.

> Anon.
> *The Stars and Stripes*
> (11 April 1919)

Joyce Kilmer

Today the Sixty-ninth parades—
I cannot see them through the trees.

The trees who lift their arms in thanks
That those they love have wandered back,
And call a benediction down
Upon the ones who stayed behind
To guard the trees of France.

The trees who through the winter days
Unbendingly present their arms,
The trees who stand so firmly there,
The thin line of eternity.
Not snow nor rain can wash from them
Their certain immortality.

The Sixty-ninth parades today—
I cannot see them through the trees.

                        Anon.
                        The Stars and Stripes
                        (16 May 1919)

5 The Shores of Home

The men of the AEF, typical of soldiers of any age, thought often of home and the things that they missed there. One soldier recalled the joys of Christmas at home. Another, if he is to be believed, fondly remembered the subway. Yet another reminisced about a former simple pleasure:

> Twenty pledges would I sign
> And forego all shades of wine
> Just to get a chance to draw
> Choc'late sody through a straw.
>
> Anon.
> *The Stars and Stripes*
> (22 March 1918)

Christmas, the subway, and even chocolate sodas would, of course, be there when the men returned. Unfortunately, the bar, the tavern, the barkeeps, and other familiar associations were being swept aside by triumphant prohibitionists. The doughboys were hardly pleased and often poetically assessed the tragedy, plumbing its depths, measuring its magnitude.

If discouraged by such developments, the men nevertheless soldiered on, well aware of their mission; and many poems indicated their own determination to see things through. Lt.

Grantland Rice, in his poem, *"Peace—And the A.E.F.,"* eloquently addressed this matter.

Having seen their goals accomplished, the men hoped to give home their undivided attention and leave France, or, if in Germany, bid a "Farewell to Coblenz" and head westward to the familiar spots of home and the re-establishment of a settled life, intending never again to roam.

The Christmas Call

*Far above the crash of conflict, ere the star
     shells flecked the morning,
     And we answered with defiance for the cause
     we love and know,
In our memory crept a picture of a day long
     since forgotten,
     And we thought of Grandma's turkey, and
     the Christmas tree, and snow.*

*We have slogged along the highways, we have
     heard adventure calling;
     We have banished dreams of comfort as we
     toyed with Fate each day;
Still across the red horizon, as the cold, gray
     dusk is falling,
     Stalks a vision of our kid days, and of
     Santa and his sleigh.*

Cpl. Howard A. Herty
The Stars and Stripes
(20 December 1918)

To The Subway

I used to ride you every night
At five or maybe six;
And every night I used to say
I'd rather ride the Styx.

I was shoved and pushed and stepped on,
I was elbowed, jostled and jammed;
It used to take a chunk off me
Each time that side door slammed.

But though I used to curse you,
I'd pay a million fare
To hear the guard yell out tonight;
"Forty-Second Street—Times Square!"

> Anon.
> *The Stars and Stripes*
> (3 May 1918)

As Things Are

The old home State is drier now
Than forty-seven clucks
Of forty-seven desert hens
'A-chewin' peanut shucks.

There everybody's standin' sad
Beside the Fishhill store,
'A-sweatin' dust an' spittin' rust
Because there ain't no more.

The constable, they write, has went
A week without a pinch.
There ain't no jobs, so there's a gent
'At sure has got a cinch.

I ain't a-gonna beef a bit,
But still, it's kinda nice,
'A-knowin' where there's some to git
Without requestin' twice.

                    Anon.
                    The Stars and Stripes
                    (26 July 1918)

Drink To Me Only

Drink to me only with thine eyes
  (Though God made them to wink with);
It's "Taps" at last for Scotch and ryes
  And things we used to drink with.
O Land, thou once were Paradise
  Of liquoring and wat'ring places;
What made the Councils of the Wise
  Transform you into an oasis?

Drink to me only with thine eyes
  (Though they were made for flashing);
The corpse of Johnnie Walker lies
  With others just as dashing
Beneath the faded Edelweiss.
  O Land, we ask, don't thusly shame us,
Bring back schooners—largest size—
  Of that which made Milwaukee famous!

Drink to me only with thine eyes
  (Though they were made for sleeping);
Deep in the dusk are longing sighs
  Of kindred spirits vigil keeping.

O Land, revoke that law which tries,
    Without appropriate explanations,
To let your Councils of the Wise
    Put Carrie in the League of Nations!*

>   Anon.
>   *The Stars and Stripes*
>   (7 February 1919)

---

* A reference to Carry Amelia Nation (1846-1911), the famous militant American temperance leader. The poet has misspelled *Carry*.

Peace—And The A. E. F.

They know, deep in their dreams,
Peace and its ancient thrills;
Peace by the singing streams,
Peace in the lonely hills;
But out from the battle hue
Here is their answer spun—
"Not till the game is through!
Not till the fight is won!"

Deep in the bitter strife,
Swept by the endless roar,
They know what they've missed of life
From years that have gone before;
But answering, gun for gun,
Here is their last call due—
"Not till the game is won!
Not till the fight is through!"

On where the crosses grow,
On where their lost mates sleep,
They drive for the waiting foe
Out where the night is deep;
Out through the crash and din

Here is their answer spun—
"Not till the score is in!
Not till the game is won!"

They know where the home fires wait,
Far from the flaring light;
They see, in the grip of Fate,
Peace and the quiet night;
Peace and the dreams they knew—
Peace and the friendly sun—
But not till the game is through!
Not till the fight is won!

                     Lt. Grantland Rice
                     The Stars and Stripes
                     (5 July 1918)

Farewell To Coblenz

*O, Coblenz Town's a fine town, and Coblenz
    sights are rare,
And Coblenz wine is good wine as one
    gets anywhere,
And smoothly runs the world there, but
    stagnant grows the mind,
And Coblenz Town of all towns I'm glad
    to leave behind.*

*Then, Ho, for Brest and transport, and
    dragging days at sea;
For though the days be long ones, they're
    welcome days to me.
The leaves are brown at home now—it's
    Indian Summer there;
The Harvest Sun is shining, through
    hazy, autumn air.*

*O, Coblenz maids are fair maids, as
    Deutscher madchens go,
But there are maidens fairer in a fairer
    land I know,*

And there are maidens truer, in the land
    where I would be,
For one I know is waiting for her doughboy,
    oversea.

Then, Hey, for crowded box-car, with
    men jammed to the door,
Where no spare inch is wasted and your
    bunk's the wooden floor,
And later on, below decks, with dizzy,
    sea-sick brain,
Your thoughts are cheery, happy thoughts
    —When You Get Home Again!

Yes, Coblenz town's a fine town, as towns
    in Europe go,
But give me towns to westward, where
    life moves not so slow,
With fewer castles, maybe,—more future
    and less past,
And then I'll give up roaming, and settle
    down at last.

"Deauboie"
The Amaroc News
(31 August 1919)

6 Les Femmes

Certainly, the girls back home were frequently on the minds of the troops abroad, sometimes with interesting consequences as 1st Lt. Harry Parker observes in his amusing poem "Left Behind." No matter how enticing the girls in Europe were, most of the soldiers were determined to be faithful and eventually to return to their American sweethearts.

Not all of the girls waited patiently, though. Sgt. Maj. Howard Herty had few doubts that *his* girl was fully occupied in his absence, and one anonymous soldier, in his amusing "To The Guy Who Landed Her," had a sad tale to tell indeed. The "Dear John" letter of World War II renown hardly originated in that conflict. One unknown poet in his "Your Soldier" lectured the wayward females, urging them to be true since he was primarily fighting for them. They should be duly impressed with the sacrifices and sufferings made on their account.

Naturally the men could be tempted too as the poem "Flashing Eyes" suggests. And if the men were enticed by the women of France, at least one writer was incensed that they were frequently viewed as all the same: women of easy virtue. Surely not all of the women were of this ilk, and the poem "The Women of France" sought to set the record straight.

If the doughboys of the AEF shared with soldiers of other wars many of their views regarding women, they did not on one score: the attitude toward their mothers. The numerous poems addressed to mothers, which appeared in both *The Stars and Stripes* and *The Amaroc News,* were much too filled with sentiments of unabashed and unashamed love for the taste of soldiers of a later date. R.C. Kyle's "Little Mother" is typical.

The troops sent to Germany initially encountered obstacles in meeting German women as 2d Lt. William Ruggles of *The Amaroc News* staff reveals in a poem in his series "Studies in Nude Life," concerned with the official attitude toward non-fraternization. There was one woman in the American occupation zone in Germany, however, perhaps an American lass, who apparently turned her share of heads. Ruggles speculated about her no doubt well-filled social schedule in his "Deferring to an Anonymous Tip." In fact, she remains an intriguing person, and one wonders whether Ruggles ever met her, somewhere in old Coblenz perhaps. One somehow hopes that he did.

Left Behind

*I got a letter from
My girl. She said,
"I love you.
When the mud is
Thick, and
You have a large pack on
Your back
And you are hungry
And tired
Think of me.
I love you."
And one day we were
On the march.
The mud was
Thick. And
I had a large
Pack
On my back
And I was
Hungry
And tired, when
I fell to thinking
Of her.*

And
A lieutenant
Gave me
A swift kick
And set me to
Double timing
To
Catch up.

                                        1st Lt. Harry L. Parker
                                        The Stars and Stripes
                                        (14 March 1919)

My Sweetheart

I left her one day and hurried away
    To answer Democracy's call;
A tear dimmed her eye as I kissed her goodbye,
    And she swore she loved me above all.

This sweetheart of mine, a vision divine,
    Was the fairest that heaven could send;
And though I did grieve, she made me believe,
    She'd be faithful to me to the end.

Does she dance with joy when some other boy
    Says, "Dearie, let's go to a show"?
Does she jump with glee and say "Come sit near
        me"*
    On the sofa that I used to know?

Don't think that I fear, when she's so sincere;
    She is, for she vowed she would be,
Does she go out nights and take in the sights?
    She does! you can take it from me!

                  Regimental Sgt. Maj.
                  Howard A. Herty
                  The Stars and Stripes
                  (21 February 1919)

To The Guy Who Landed Her (A Piece of Very Free Verse)

Yes, she wrote me the other day
All about it;
Said she saw a lot in you that she never saw before,
Said I'd done you an injustice in the things I said about you,
Added that I had been careless in writing to her,
(Which is the postal department's fault, and not mine),
And said she didn't think I cared for her any more.
Result: She's engaged to you!

Well, congratulations!
There never was a finer girl in all the world,
And, probably, there never will be!
In short, you are a whole lot luckier than,
In all due respect, you deserve to be.

I could have married her last April
Before the selective service law went into effect,
And then the War Department could have whistled for me
And been out of luck for its whistling.
But I wasn't going to get tied up with any woman,
No matter how fine she was, with a war like this one a-gcing,

*So I enlisted, and she thought it great.
She called me hero, brave boy, all the rest,
Knit sweaters for me, and made wristlets for me,
And came down to see me in camp.*

*I thought, of course, that it was all fine stuff,
That I'd come back at least a sergeant-major
With a* Croix de Guerre, *a medal of honor and all that,
And a big* pickelhaube *helmet to put on the mantelpiece
To use as the baby's bank.*

*But no such luck. I wrote her, just like clockwork,
Stinted myself on beer to buy her handkerchiefs,
Kept lights after taps to look at her picture,
And, any way you've a mind to take it, played it square.
I didn't learn French, for the simple reason
That I didn't want to get in with any French dames
And so be tempted to forget her.
But that's all the good it did me—you're It now,
And all my joining up has gone for nothing.*

*Oh, I don't care; I've got a job before me—
It doesn't bring in as much money as yours does,
But it's a damn sight more interesting;
And I don't have to take out insurance for anyone
Unless I want to.
I guess when I get back things will be different
And I'll make up, in job-getting, what you have gained
By not going to war at all.*

No, I'm not sore or sour-grapes, or anything,
But I just want to let you know I'm on to you—
I know you're 32, and past the draft age;
I know that, even if they boosted the draft age,
You'd plead an aged mother to support
(Whom you haven't given a cent to in the last five years).

Oh, you're within the law, all right; no one can blame you,
With such a prize before you, for popping the question
And getting her to agree to marry you.
In fact, to take it from a world point of view,
She'd be a fool if she didn't.

BUT—
When we get back, all full of prunes and glory,
I don't want to see you, cheering, on the sidewalk,
I don't want to receive your congratulations,
Nor to be invited to your house for dinner
To meet Her and the kids—oh, no!
Because I've got my opinion of a guy
That'll let another guy go out and defend his home for him
(And run the chance of dying for defending him)
And just about as much as threaten a girl into marrying him—
And don't you forget it!

                              Anon.
                              The Stars and Stripes
                              (15 March 1918)

Your Soldier

It is for you. Through endless nights
Of mud and rain he stubbornly
Plods on, head down, back bent beneath
His pack—on towards the shell-streaked sky
And maddening roar where truth and lies
And love and hate and life and death
All meet in war, red war! He loves
And hates, and so he fights. To all
His love be true. Guard well your heart
And keep the faith. He fights for you!

                              Anon.
                              The Stars and Stripes
                              (22 November 1918)

Flashing Eyes

Flashing eyes that tempt and taunt me,
  Are you never tranquil, pray?
Think you those gay glances daunt me,
Or that I don't know you want me
  To remain in France alway?
Think you that they'll ever haunt me
  If I do not stay?

Flashing eyes, could I but try it,
  I should whisper words that may
Turn those cheeks where dimples diet
Into fields where roses riot
  On a summer day;
Flashing eyes, won't you be quiet?
  Love may lose the way!

Anon.
The Stars and Stripes
(31 January 1919)

The Women of France

Who is it has slandered the women of France,
    Calling them every one cocotte,
Saying they lived for license, romance?
    He who has known them not;
Who never has sounded the peasant's heart,
Nor those who live in the higher part,
The souls that are noble, the lives that are art—
    The wonderful women of France.

These modern Spartans by stern toil worn,
    Back of the men who face the grave;
The men out there by these women borne—
    And these women more than the men are brave.
The sons of these mothers at Verdun stood—
Can decadent women such men brood?
Nay, only the holy, steadfast, good—
    The marvelous mothers of France.

Who is it has slandered the women of France?
    He who looks for the lower kind,

Who only for fallen has room in his glance—
    "As ye seek, so shall ye find."

> Anon.
> *The Stars and Stripes*
> (6 September 1918)

Little Mother

I am writing this little poem
    To the mother I left behind,
And it tells of my longing for her
    Over here in the daily grind.

I am often alone and lonely
    On a post out in No Man's Land,
But my thoughts they go floating homeward
    To my mother in dreams so grand.

I dream of you again, dear mother,
    As you bade me that last goodbye,
And I marched, a proud Yankee soldier,
    For my country to do or die.

Countless days have passed since we parted,
    Weary days of hard toil and pain,
But my visions of you have cheered me
    As I fancy your face again.

How I long for your smiles of gladness
    That are haunting my mem'ry still,

And the love in your eyes beseeching
    Even now makes my pulses thrill.

How you held me with hands so gentle,
    Closely pressed to your throbbing breast;
In that last fond embrace I promised
    To live true through the crucial test.

The caress of your hair, soft silver,
    On my cheek how I fain would feel,
And from lips that are soft as roses,
    A sweet kiss I would like to steal.

Little mother, for you there's burning
    A deep love that will never die,
Spurring on to the fight before us
    Where the Angel of Death doth fly.

Oh, it may be that only in Heaven
    I will meet you again, mother, dear,
But it matters not what befalls me—
    The bright star of your love shines clear.

                    R. C. Kyle
                    The Stars and Stripes
                    (10 May 1918)

Studies in Nude Life

*She wore a pink silk blazer and her hair
    was wavy brown,
And a naughty little twinkle made me
    chase her through the town;
She was shy and quite elusive—but not too
    shy, I think—
So I'm sweeping Coblenz gutters and I'm
    rusting in the clink.*

*There was music in her laughter as it lilted
    through the air—
Her eyes were winking mischief—a delusion
    and a snare:
It was spring—my heart went hurdling to
    its age-old whisperings
So I'm charged with fraternizing and a
    dozen other things.*

*I was "strolling mit a fraulein" I'd my
    "arm around her waist"
And I "smacked an M.P. sergeant," which
    is not in best of taste*

I was "peddling Q.M. sales stuff," which
    is chocolate, no less—
Oh, the charge sheet's pretty nifty and I'm
    resting in duress.

Oh, it's not the jug I'm filling nor the gobs
    they'll take of pay,
Nor the thirty days' hard labor that I know
    the court will say:
It's that nifty pink silk blazer and the
    twinkle in her eyes—
And the fact that M.P. nabbed me—ere—
    I—could—fraternize.

                              2d Lt. William B. Ruggles
                              The Amaroc News
                              (14 May 1919)

Deferring to an Anonymous Tip

("Calling your attention to the fact that Miss — has the only pair of purple dancing pumps in the A. of O."* Letter to Editor).

*Fades the grumble of the Berthas, the
    machine gun's sputter fails—
The memory of old hardships and of
    weary marches pales:
They may live in retrospection, but our
    thoughts in rapture jumps,
As the tinkling patter rises of those purple
    dancing pumps.*

*We could rhyme on hob-nailed field shoes
    with their blisters, corns and pain—
Russetts, cordovans and puttees would not
    summon us in vain;
But there are thoughts where words are
    failures and our inspiration stumps,
As we conjure up the vision of those purple
    dancing pumps.*

*Little brogans, whisper to us where you
    pass your nights away—
Will you step to boots of colonels or to
    privates' clogs today?*

---

* A. of O. stands for Army of Occupation, i.e., the American forces on duty in Germany.

*We are tired of rough-neck rhyming—all
    our old ambition slumps—
We would bring it back by waltzing to a
    pair of purple pumps.*

*Talismans of Cinderella, while She dances
    light and gay,
May your leather last forever as she trips
    along life's way—
Through our dull drab days will twinkle, as
    our heart-beats miss their thumps,
A pair of gray silk ankles and the purple
    dancing pumps.*

> 2d Lt. William B. Ruggles
> *The Amaroc News*
> (22 May 1919)

7 Allies and Enemies

One can almost see them now, as the troopships slowly steam into Brest or some other French port, the men on deck straining to catch their first glimpse of the French coast, their first overseas goal. Breathed sighs of relief were mingled with the eagerness and excitement; they had foiled the subs. Their first contacts with French soil were probably not the most attractive, however, as they soon marched away from the ships to the dreary, muddy camps nearby. Only later would they obtain fleeting glimpses of the beautiful French countryside, probably through the doors of the famous "40 and 8" boxcars of (to the Americans) the ludicrous tiny French trains. Meanwhile, the men were already struggling with the French language, an effort in which most were doomed to defeat, though some developed a commendable fluency. Others, of Franco-American stock, hailing perhaps from such cities as New Orleans, spoke the language; but far more men of the AEF spoke German rather than French as their second—or first—language. German would come in handy only after the war by those finding themselves detailed to occupation duty in the defeated Reich, though while hostilities were underway, the men were forbidden to speak German at all.

But if the men were not fluent in the French tongue, they certainly picked up some of the words, among the first "mastered" being the ubiquitous "toot sweet," though 2d Lt.

John Roche, as his poem "I Love You" suggests, mastered other words.

If the language was amusing or exasperating, what the French suffered in the war, or hoped to obtain from it, could not fail to make a deep impression on the Americans. When he encountered French civilians in "A Little Town Where We Rested," Cpl. Russell Lord, for instance, gained determination to carry on the battle.

Many accounts of the days following the Armistice mention the large numbers of captured German guns that the French placed on display in Paris. These trophies provided a backdrop for the peace negotiations that began in the French capital in January of 1919. Paul L. Evans poetically reflected on what the guns symbolized, while expressing his hopes that the Great Crusade had stilled their vicious bark forever.

Regarding their enemies, the doughboys, at least poetically, almost never mentioned Austria-Hungary, Turkey or Bulgaria, the other members of the Central Powers. There was only one enemy worthy of their steel: Germany, the detested symbol of which was, of course, the Kaiser, with his equally hated son the Crown Prince coming in for his share of abuse. Truly, the Kaiser, "The Lord of Villainy," was to most Americans, fit only for the harshest punishment for the grief he had caused the world.

I Love You

I've heard a lot of music
    As a connoisseur of tone
I've harkened to the operas
    And the moaning saxophone.
I've listened to the jazzers
    When they did their raggy worst,
But for harmony that's scrumptious
    I know I heard it first
When Yvonne, la plus jolie,
Said, as she looked at me,
    "Je vous aime!"

The ginks who play on glasses,
    And ring the shiny chimes,
Or the organ at the movies—
    I've heard them lots of times,
And the Wops who play the zither,
    And accordian to Hoyle,
Have left my ears a-tingle,
    But they never touched the soul
Like Marie, qui est belle,
When she whispered, ah, so well,
    "Je vous adore!"

I've heard John Philip Sousa
    Play all his famous stuff,
And the art of the Victrola
    Has lured me oft enough;
But though I give them credit
    In their amateurish way,
When it comes to downright music
    I heard it first that day,
When Odette, ma cherie,
Murmured tenderly,
        "Je t'aime!"

                                  2d Lt. John Pierre Roche
                                  The Stars and Stripes
                                  (15 November 1918)

Lines On Leaving A Little Town Where We Rested

We with the war ahead,
 You who have held the line,
Laughing, have broken bread
 And taken wine.

We cannot speak your tongue,
 We cannot fully know
Things hid beneath your smile
 Four years ago.

Things which have given us,
 Grimly, a common debt,
Now that we take the field
 We won't forget!

> Cpl. Russell Lord
> *The Stars and Stripes*
> (6 September 1918)

The Captured Guns

*In Paris streets the captured guns in frowning
    silence stand;*
*Broken, unlimbered, torn and rent, encumbering
    the land.*
*Spawned of malice, sired of hate—to hell con-
    signed they are—*
*As France, triumphant, leaps from them to her
    ascending star.*

*Now little ones can pat these guns and ride upon
    their snouts;*
*They can play at games among them with child-
    ish screams and shouts.*
But sadly does the poilu pause—and bitter is his
    thought—*
*To him, they are the symbols of a hundred
    battles fought.*

*To him, they grimly represent a million graves
    up there,*
*His crippled, blinded comrades, the wail of world
    despair.*

* French soldier.

*He knows the price to bring those guns to rest
 on Paris streets—
The price in blood, the blasted homes, the march-
 ings and retreats.*

*He knows the price that France must pay
 throughout the years ahead;
How all that live must render their accounting
 to the dead—
The dead that died with Christ to bring a Resur-
 rection Morn;
The dead to whom all men must bow for Liberty
 reborn.*

*And yet it is most fitting—and it was for this
 they died—
That boys and girls might play and romp, and
 run about and hide;
That mothers looking on may know that these
 subjected guns
Mute standing tell the end of war, the safety of
 their sons.*

Paul L. Evans
The Stars and Stripes
(30 May 1919)

The Lord of Villainy

*Captain Kidd played the pirate game, but he
 played it on the square;
He never sunk ships with babes on board and
 let them founder there;
He did some hefty robbing, and his acting
 sure was crass,
But he never once resorted to the use of
 poison gas.
Robin Hood played the robber game, but he
 played it handsome, too;
He bled the fat and wealthy, but he let the
 poor right through.
He never took indemnities from those who
 were in need,
But rustic Robin had no chance to learn the
 Teuton creed.
Henry Morgan roamed the Main as a down-
 right buccaneer,
He guzzled on Jamaica rum, and never stooped
 to beer;
He was a downright lowbrow, a roughneck,
 Heaven knows,—*

*But hist'ry doesn't say that Hank e'er cru-
    cified his foes.
Alexander (called the Great) set out to rule
    the world;
Against each peaceful nation his phalanxes
    were hurled.
"He saw and took"; but when he'd got the
    thing he most desired,
He didn't lie about it, and make honest
    people tired.
Villains they were of ancient days, each in
    his separate line,
But it remains for Wilhelm all their vices
    to combine
And add some new ones of his own—his
    crimes on land and sea
Have branded him forever as the Lord of
    Villainy.*

Anon.
The Stars and Stripes
(22 February 1918)

8 The Lighter Side: Laughs and Levity

The Stars and Stripes and *The Amaroc News* were nothing if not humorous sheets. This is not surprising when one considers that among their functions was that of elevating troop morale. But even without that mission, the papers would no doubt have reflected the high good humor of the AEF, made up as it was of high-spirited young men on an exciting adventure, looking at the world with open, clear-eyed countenance and never-say-die attitude. There was something of the "Laughing Cavalier" about the American Expeditionary Forces.

To infantrymen, the catchy "Yes, There Is Rest," must have brought smiles, and common occurrences of daily army life were the objects of fun even if more or less serious in reality. Inspections were a common bane, for instance, especially for those perennially unprepared, and every outfit certainly had at least one resident "goldbrick" who was invariably caught short. Pvt. Edwin Underhill's recounting of one man's dilemma can still produce a grin or two. Then, too, the watchwords of the Great Crusade roused many to the battle, but they could become frayed as an anonymous poet insisted in his "Canned War Cries." Songs especially lent themselves to parodies, and certain tunes seemed particularly funny, at least in special contexts. The story was recounted in the 30 August 1918 issue of *The Stars and Stripes* of one platoon of American doughboys who emerged from a wood about a mile south of the Vesle River singing "They Go Wild, Simply Wild Over Me!", referring to a company of Germans "who were running toward Germany across the open field in front of the wood." Far behind the lines, in the area of the S.O.S. [Services of Supply], another song seemed even more appropriate, if its words were suitably changed, so as to respond to the anticipated questions regarding how dangerous things had been at the front. The ranks of the AEF were not lacking in lyricists either. Some pieces of music, though, were apparently heard far too often, including "It's A Long, Long Trail," and the provocative "Keep Your Head Down, Allemand," a particularly characteristic piece of bravado and bombast.

Yes, There Is Rest

Of all the animals alive
I'd rather be the bear;
He gets a full meal once a year,
And never cuts his hair—(I tell you).

Chorus: Yes, there is rest, yes, there is rest;
In the Infantree—
In the Infantree—YOU SAID IT!
Yes, there is rest,
Yes, there is rest,
In the Infantree there is rest,
SWEET REST!

Of all the fish that swim the lakes
I'd rather be the pike;
They have no bathing problem and
They drink whene'er they like—(I tell you).

Of all the barnyard fowls I know,
The rooster is the best;
He blows his own sweet reveille,
Then goes back to his nest—(I tell you).

The General has his motor car,
The Colonel has his horse;
Whenever they see doughboys hike,
It fills them with remorse (?)—(I tell you).

The First Loot wears his silver bars,
The Second Loot's are gold;
But when the Skipper comes around,
They do just as they're told—(I tell you).

The Sergeant can report you for
A gun all caked with rust;
But if his own gun's dirty, why,
The Sergeant will be bust—(I tell you).

                              Anon.
                              The Stars and Stripes
                              (21 June 1918)

The Goldbrick Stands Inspection

There is trouble in the air,
Soldiers busy everywhere—
I'm wondering what makes them act that way.
I think I have a hunch,
From the actions of the bunch,
There's a show-down inspection due today.

I wish they'd let me rest,
I should worry how I'm dressed,
These inspections keep a man upon the run.
My equipment I must find,
If I don't I'll be confined.
It's been a week since I have cleaned my gun.

Oh, the worry and the strain,
Upon my wearied brain!
I wonder where my O.D. shirt can be?
A pair of socks are missing,
It sure does keep me guessing,
Keeping up with my equipment C.*

Hobnails must be well oiled,
My uniform unsoiled,

---

* Equipment C was the American soldier's basic clothing and paraphernalia issue. It had to be displayed in good condition at inspections.

And I've only got an hour to get them clean.
    It will take all day and night
    To clean my rifle right,
And I know the C. O.'s eyes are mighty keen.

    My mess-kit is a wreck,
    I will get it in the neck.
There is rust upon my knife and fork and spoon.
    Well, I'll take another chance—
    They may pass without a glance,
I hope the war is over pretty soon.

    The Top has called us out.
    "Inspection Arms" he shouts;
And up my back there slowly creeps a chill.
    The C. O. takes my gun—
    My confinement has begun,
Now I'm serving my enlistment in the Mill.

                                Pvt. Edwin H. Underhill
                                The Stars and Stripes
                                (31 January 1919)

Canned War Cries

If anybody tells me that he's out "to can the Kaiser,"
If any one should mention "driving Fritzy o'er the Rhine,"
Right at his epiglottis in a moment I would fly, sir—
No guy so unoriginal can be a friend of mine!
"The rocky road to Berlin" and "the fight of Might 'gainst Right,"
Such sentiments, repeated oft by lecturers and such,
Will drive me in a frenzy out into the shelly night,
With the fond hope of acquiring a wooden limb or crutch!

"Do our bit" and "do our darnedest," "slacker," "bomb-proof" and the rest
Of the hackneyed war-terms bore me like a bullet from the Boche;
"Crown the Crown Prince!" "Bean the Bertha"—oh, they're all a blooming pest,
And if they don't stop saying 'em, I'll squeal to General Foch.
"Ships will win the war, and aeros,"—I have heard that line before;
"They shall not pass"—I weary of the finest of the bunch!
They all were grand the first time, but, repeated o'er and o'er,
The best of war-time slogans sure is bound to lose its punch.

Can't they issue us new sayings as they issue us new pants?
Can't they put originality in patriotic spiels?
Can't they think up something peppy, new, to get the boys in France,

Or are we to be handed out the same old verbal deals?
Our grub's the same from day to day, our clothes are all one cut,
Our drills, and our policing with monotony are rife;
Oh, I wish on those old war-cries that the trap-door firm would
     shut—
They were great once; but variety's the spice of Army life!

                        Anon.
                        The Stars and Stripes
                        (28 June 1918)

(Untitled)*

And when they ask us
How dangerous it was,
    We never will tell them,
    We never will tell them.
We spent our pay
    In some café,
And fought wild women
    Night and day—
'Twas the awfullest war we ever knew.
And when they ask us
(And they're certainly going to ask us)
Just why it was we did not win the Croix de Guerre,
    We never will tell them,
    We never will tell them—
There was a front, but damned if we knew where.

                      Anon.
                      The Stars and Stripes
                      (24 January 1919)

---

*   Sung to the tune of "They Wouldn't Believe Me."

"And The Only Tune—"

Mary Young, who's come to stay,
Plays the piano at the "Y" all day;
And the only tune she's beaten frail
Is that picked on "It's a Long, Long Trail."

Tom, Tom, in the next door billet,
Sings all night till we holler "Kill it!"
He gives us more than we can stand
Of "Keep your head down, Allemand."

                      Anon.
                      The Stars and Stripes
                      (31 May 1918)

9 A Miscellany

The close ties between buddies was one well-known feature of AEF life. Lifelong friends were formed in the war experience. Not surprisingly, poets turned their attention to this facet of army life, among them being Pvt. Miles O'Reilly, whose "The Canteen" captures the feeling of comradeship. This is an authentic voice opposing the far less realistic strains of the lugubrious song "My Buddy," which many doughboys scorned.

Those close ties which were also commemorated in poetry were often forged on the various fields of battle entwined with the AEF's history. Who could forget the role that the River Marne played in the Great War? Certainly not the readers of the poems of Sgt. Frank Carraugh, who wrote his "The Fields of the Marne" shortly before he died of battle wounds. A Sgt. Fair recalled the feelings of men marching to those battlefields in his "Back To The Line," and an unknown poet captured something of the quickening pace of events in the spring of 1918 in his jaunty "Spring."

Several poems graphically reveal the thoughts of soldiers forced to think seriously, perhaps for the first time, by what they were experiencing. Rather lighter is *The Stars and Stripes'* staffer Pvt. Hudson Hawley's "Just Thinking." William Gilligan's "The Night Is Done" is more profound.

The World War I poem "In Flanders Fields," by John

McCrae, is the most famous of the "poppy poems." The symbolism of the poppies on the battlefield proved too much for many poets to resist. The Americans, especially at Château-Thierry, had fought and died in poppies—and in wheat. The haunting "Through the Wheat," by an anonymous poet, and Capt. John Hanson's "Poppies" are worthy of standing beside McCrae's much better known piece.

With the ending of the war, the men turned towards home, planning how they would pick up the pieces of their lives. Many men sought simply to return to "normalcy," the buzzword soon to be current at home. A poem by one veteran, Albert Jay Cook, well illustrates those intentions. His creation "After The War" might be regarded as a poetic precursor to Hemingway's 1925 story, "Big Two-Hearted River," the hero of which, Nick Adams, returning after the war, sought peace and restoration of soul and body in the wilderness.

Yet lurking behind the facade of such contentment was the disillusionment of the later 1920s. Maj. Guy Kindersley's "The Shepherds Feed Themselves And Feed Not My Flock" was therefore a harbinger of the literary flood to come.

The Canteen

There are bonds of all sorts in this world
of ours,
Fetters of friendship, and ties of flowers,
And true lovers' knots, I ween;
The boy and the girl are bound by a kiss,
But there's never a bond, old friend, like
this,—
We have drunk from the same canteen!

It was sometimes water and sometimes
milk
And sometimes applejack, fine as silk,
But, whatever the tipple has been,
We shared it together, in bane or bliss,
And I warm to you, friend, when I think
of this—
We have drunk of the same canteen!

The rich and the great sit down to dine,
And they quaff to each other in sparkling
wine,
From glasses of crystal and green;

But I guess in their golden potations
             they miss
The warmth of regard to be found in
             this,—
      We have drunk from the same canteen!

We have shared our blankets and tents
             together,
And have marched and fought in all
             kinds of weather,
      And hungry and full we have been;
Had days of battle and days of rest,
But this memory I cling to and love the
             best,—
      We have drunk of the same canteen!

For when wounded I lay on the outer
             slope.
With my blood flowing fast, and but
             little hope
      Upon which my faint spirit could lean,
O then, I remember, you crawled to my
             side,
And, bleeding so fast it seemed both must
             have died,
      We have drunk from the same canteen!

                                    Pvt. Miles O'Reilly
                                    The Amaroc News
                                    (10 December 1921)

The Fields Of The Marne

The fields of the Marne are growing green,
The river murmurs on and on;
No more the hail of mitrailleuse*
The cannon from the hills are gone.

The herder leads the sheep afield,
Where grasses grow o'er broken blade;
And toil-worn women till the soil
O'er human mold, in sunny glade.

The splintered shell and bayonet
Are lost in crumbling village wall;
No sniper scans the rim of hills,
No sentry hears the night bird call.

From blood-wet soil and sunken trench,
The flowers bloom in summer light;
And farther down the vale beyond,
The peasant smiles are sad, yet bright.

The wounded Marne is growing green,
The gash of Hun no longer smarts;

---

*   Machine guns.

*Democracy is born again,
But what about the wounded hearts?*

> Sgt. Frank Carraugh
> *The Stars and Stripes*
> (16 August 1918)

Back To The Line

Trampin' along through the darkness,
    Splashin' my way through the rain,
With a chafin' pack slung on my back,
    Bound for the trenches again.

Flashes of light in the distance,
    Splotches o' red on the sky,
The sound of a shell creatin' hell
    In a convoy creepin' by.

Our line moves on like a shadow
    Pushin' its way through the wreck,
Each man in his place, rain in his face
    And streamin' cold down his neck.

Silent and grave, movin' forward,
    Each havin' thoughts all his own,
As we tramp the path o' the War Lord's wrath
    Where the fires o' hell are blown.

Dreamin' o' home an' the old folks,
    An' the fields o' yellow grain,
An' the old rock spring, an' everything—
    Bound for the trenches again.

                Sgt. Fair
                The Stars and Stripes
                (10 January 1919)

Spring

It's Spring at home; I know the signs—
The buds are bursting on the vines,
The birds speed high with happier wings,
The heart of youth is glad, and sings.

It's Spring in France; I know the signs—
The mass of reserves behind the lines;
The heart of youth burgeons once more
To manhood, and resurgent war!

                        Anon.
                        The Stars and Stripes
                        (5 July 1918)

Just Thinking

Standin' up here on the fire-step,
Lookin' ahead in the mist,
With a tin hat over your ivory
And a rifle clutched in your fist;
Waitin' and watchin', and wond'rin'
If the Hun's comin' over tonight—
Say, aren't the things you think of
Enough to give you a fright?

Things you ain't even thought of
For a couple o' months or more;
Things that 'ull set you laughin',
Things that 'ull make you sore;
Things that you saw in the movies,
Things that you saw on the street,
Things that you're really proud of,
Things that are—not so sweet.

Debts that are past collectin',
Stories you hear and forget,
Ball games and birthday parties,
Hours of drill in the wet;
Headlines, recruitin' posters,

Sunsets 'way out at sea,
Evenings of pay days—golly—
It's a queer thing, this memory!

Faces of pals in Homeburg,
Voices of women folk,
Verses you learnt in schooldays
Pop up in the mist and smoke.
As you stand there, grippin' that rifle,
A-starin', and chilled to the bone,
Wonderin' and wonderin' and wonderin',
Just thinkin' there—all alone!

When will the war be over?
When will the gang break through?
What will the U. S. look like?
What will there be to do?
Where will the Boches be then?
Who will have married Nell?
When's that relief a-comin' up?
Gosh! But this thinkin's hell!

Pvt. Hudson Hawley
The Stars and Stripes
(15 February 1918)

The Night Is Done

Some whispered words, and then I was alone
In the vast temple of the Night;
How much it seemed like early youth
When darkness holds a myriad crouching forms—
Another infancy.

Now and then crashed into the solemn harmony
        of the stars,
In high staccato notes, some animated gun;
Or ghastly complained against the night some
        ghoulish flare,
Lingering and dying in the air,
Silence and dark return.

Again the stars, unnumbered save by an infinity,
And each perhaps a solar scheme,
Now following a hopeless course of grim fatality,
As I.

But what is death to them? How do they die?
Death!—'twas not a noise—'twas just imagination.
If senseless form and motion have no end,
Why then should I?

And their beginning, 'ere the nebulae—
If mystery enshroud the first, why not the last?—

A friendly sound; some whispered words, Relief.
The night is done.

William Gilligan
The Stars and Stripes
(15 November 1918)

Through the Wheat (The Sergeant's Story)

"There's a job out there before us,"
    Said the Captain, kinder solemn;
"There's a crop out there to gather
    Through the wheat fields just ahead."
Through the wheat of Château-Thierry
    That was soon to hold our column,
"There's a crop out there to gather,"
    That was all the Captain said.
(Oh, at dawn, the wheat was yellow,
    But at night the wheat was red.)

"There's a crop out there to gather"—
    And we felt contentment stealin'
Like a ghost from out the shadows
    Of a lost, old-fashioned street;
For the crop out there before us
    Brought a kinder home-like feelin',
Though the zippin' German bullets
    Started hissin' through the wheat.
But it didn't seem to bother
    As we slogged along the beat.

"There's snakes here," whooped a private
    As the bullets started hissin';

And we saw that Hun machine guns
    In the thicket formed our crop;
So we started for the harvest
    Where a bunch of them was missin',
But a bunch of them was hittin'
    Where we hadn't time to stop.
But we damned 'em to a finish
    As we saw a bunkie drop.

So we gathered in the harvest,
    And we didn't leave one missin';
(We had gathered crops before this
    With as tough a job ahead.)
Through the wheat of Château-Thierry,
    With the German bullets hissin',
"There's a crop out there to gather,"
    That was all the Captain said.
(Oh, at dawn the wheat was yellow,
    But at night the wheat was red.)

                        Anon.
                        The Stars and Stripes
                        (9 August 1918)

Poppies

*Poppies in the wheat fields on the pleasant hills
 of France.*
*Reddening in the summer breeze that bids them
 nod and dance;*
*Over them the skylark sings his lilting, liquid
 tune—*
*Poppies in the wheat fields, and all the world in
 June.*

*Poppies in the wheat fields on the road to
 Monthiers—*
*Hark, the spiteful rattle where the masked machine
 guns play!*
*Over them the shrapnel's song greets the summer
 morn—*
*Poppies in the wheat fields—but, ah, the fields
 are torn.*

*See the stalwart Yankee lads, never ones to
 blench,*
*Poppies in their helmets as they clear the
 shallow trench,*

*Leaping down the furrows with eager, boyish
    tread*
*Through the poppied wheat fields to the flaming
    woods ahead.*

*Poppies in the wheat fields as sinks the summer
    sun,*
*Broken, bruised and trampled—but the bitter
    day is won;*
*Yonder in the woodland where the flashing rifles
    shine,*
*With their poppies in their helmets, the front
    files hold the line.*

*Poppies in the wheat fields; how still beside them
    lie*
*Scattered forms that stir not when the star shells
    burst on high;*
*Gently bending o'er them beneath the moon's
    soft glance,*
*Poppies of the wheat fields on the ransomed hills
    of France.*

> Capt. John Mills Hanson
> *The Stars and Stripes*
> (6 September 1918)

After the War

Along the granite passes
    Ye will find me if ye seek—
In the ranges where the prisoned ages frown;
Beside the tumbling waters
    Fed from off a distant peak,
Where an avalanche of sky is pouring down!

Along the mirrored fringes,
    Where the shore line Norways stand,
By the silent pools that dot the northern trails;
Where God has chiseled sermons
    In his own and mighty hand,
And the loon, a jeering unbeliever, wails.

The wind that courses wildly
    Down the scented forest lanes,
I shall breathe until fairly drunken with its wines;
(Like ardent, fiery liquor
    To my jaded, slugging veins,
Is the bonny, balsam odor of the pines).

And then, surfeit with nature,
    I shall lay me down to rest

In a languid, dreamless, woodland sort of way,
As the sun is hanging pendant
    In the airways of the West
Like a medal pinned upon the breast of day!

> Albert Jay Cook
> *The Stars and Stripes*
> (18 October 1918)

The Shepherds Feed Themselves And Feed Not My Flock

*We died in our millions to serve it; the
    cause that you told us was ours,
We stood waist-deep in the trenches, we
    battled with Hell and its powers;
And you? You have gathered your millions;
    you have lined your pockets
    with pelf,
You have talked of the rights of Nations,
    while you worshipped the rights of
    self;
Do you think we shall rise and smite
    you? Fear not. You shall garner
    your gain.
And we? Will you give us our freedom,
    just those who have not been slain?
Fooled tho we've been by your hierlings
    —you know that we fought for a lie—
We fathomed a truth you see not, but one
    you must learn when you die,
That silver and gold and raiment are
    things of but little worth,*

*For Love is the heir of the ages, and the
    meek shall inherit the earth.*

> Maj. Guy M. Kindersley
> *The Amaroc News*
> (7 September 1919)